O'Doherty's Rebellion:
The London Newsbooks

Rob Dougherty

Lulu.com

© 2008 by Rob Dougherty
All rights reserved. No part of this document may be reproduced or transmitted in any form or by any means, electronic, mechanical, photocopying, recording, or otherwise, without prior permission of the author.

This book, more O'Doherty information, and related merchandise are available at www.odoherty1608.com
Contact the author at rob@odoherty1608.com

Published by Lulu.com
ISBN 978-1-4357-0861-7

Introduction

On the 18th of April, 1608, Sir Cahir O'Doherty, Lord of Inishowen, launched a rebellion against the English government that left the governor of Derry dead and the city burnt to the ground. O'Doherty fought on for several months before being killed at Doon Rock near Kilmacrenan on July 5, 1608. He was drawn and quartered, and his head was impaled on a pole and displayed in Dublin.

Three news booklets about the rebellion were printed and sold in London that year. Objective journalism they are not. There were many factors that influenced O'Doherty's actions but according to the authors of these newsbooks it was a purely unprovoked and traitorous attack against an English government that had treated O'Doherty with great respect and kindness. This book presents those three newsbooks after a brief introduction to the historical context. For a more in-depth account see *The Flight of the Earls* by John McCavitt. The Flight of the Earls was the sudden, secret departure of a number of Gaelic leaders from Ireland in 1607. It was one of a series of events leading up to O'Doherty's Rebellion. McCavitt's narrative continues through O'Doherty's Rebellion in 1608 and on to the aftermath of these two events which are considered to be the end of the old order in Ireland.

Sir Cahir O'Doherty

In 1632 a Franciscan monk from Donegal named Michael O'Clery began a four-year project to transcribe the various historical manuscripts in Ireland into a single work. The result was the *Annals of the Kingdom of Ireland* which is better known as the *Annals of the Four Masters* after the four men (including O'Clery) who compiled them. The *Annals* begin in biblical times and continue through the year 1616 so they include an account of O'Doherty's Rebellion. They also include an entry from the year 972 AD saying "Diarmaid, son of Dochartach, Abbot of Daimhinis, died." This Dochartach is the ancestor of the O'Dohertys (of all of the variant spellings.) There are various theories on the meaning of the name: stern, unlucky, hurtful, obstructive, or possibly destroyer. Another theory says that it refers to people who live in oak houses. The grandson of Dochartach and all later descendants would have been named O'Dochartach or, more commonly, O'Dochartaigh.

Dochartach was the descendant through some fourteen generations of the 4th century King of Ireland, Niall of the Nine Hostages. Niall was thought by some historians to be a "semi-mythical" figure but recent DNA research suggests otherwise. A study done at Trinity College Dublin found that men with surnames traditionally linked to Niall have Y chromosomes indicating descent from a common male ancestor who lived in the time of Niall. One in twelve men in Ireland have this chromosome and in northwestern Ireland the rate is one in five. In the group of surnames believed to be descendants of Niall it is even more common. Surnames in this group include O'Neill (for whom Niall is the namesake), O'Doherty, O'Gallagher, O'Boyle, O'Donnell, O'Connor, Cannon, Bradley, O'Reilly, Flynn, McKee, Campbell, Devlin, Donnelly, Egan, Gormley, Hynes, McCaul, McGovern, McLoughlin, McManus, McMenamin, Molloy, O'Kane, O'Rourke, and Quinn.

Sir Cahir O'Doherty was born in 1587, some twenty-five generations after Dochartach. His father was Lord of Inishowen, the northwestern most corner of Ireland. After the death of his father in 1600 Cahir became the chieftain at the age of fourteen. At the time of his rebellion and death he was twenty-one years old. The current clann chieftain is Dr. Ramon Salvador O'Dogherty of Cadiz, Spain who is descended through ten generation from John O'Doherty, the brother of Sir Cahir. Members of that branch of the family have lived in Spain since the 18th century.

The Rebellion

Why did O'Doherty rebel? The precipitating event was an argument with the Governor of Derry, Sir George Paulet, who struck O'Doherty. Sir Cahir had had a good relationship with the previous governor, Sir Henry Docwra but with the arrival of Paulet things took a turn for the worse. Paulet was no diplomat and provoked the Irish frequently. There had been previous disputes between O'Doherty and Paulet but being assaulted was apparently more than O'Doherty could tolerate.

At the turn of the 17th century the English government was determined to exert greater control in northern Ireland. The seat of government was in Dublin, in the south, leaving the remote north somewhat out of sight and out of mind. Several of the northern earls had rebelled in the Nine Years' War (1594-1603) but the O'Dohertys had sided with the English in that war. In fact, over the years O'Doherty had been cooperative with the English and had even received a knighthood. This didn't prevent his being treated with suspicion along with the more rebellious Gaelic chieftains. The English constantly suspected that conspiracies were afoot. Their fears were not always unfounded but their lack of trust guaranteed that there would be trouble.

On September 4, 1607, the Earl of Tyrone, the Earl of Tyrconnell and nearly one hundred others sailed out of Ireland in the so-called Flight of the Earls. They most likely intended to come back with military support from the King of Spain but that never developed and they never returned. The English became even more distrustful of O'Doherty as a result. He was falsely accused of starting an uprising before he actually did and he was jailed for a short time. In another incident Paulet attempted to take one of his castles. Ultimately the harassment proved too much and the assault from Paulet was the last straw.

According to the *Annals of the Four Masters*, "Great dissensions and strife arose between the Governor of Derry, Sir George Pawlett, and O'Doherty (Cahir, the son of John Oge). The Governor not only offered him insult and abuse by word, but also inflicted chastisement on his body; so that he would rather have suffered death than live to brook such insult and dishonour, or defer or delay to take revenge for it; and he was filled with anger and fury, so that he nearly ran to distraction and madness. What he did was, to consult with his friends how he should take revenge for the insult which was inflicted upon him. What they first unanimously resolved, on the 3rd of May, was to invite to him Captain Hart, who was at

Cuil-mor (a fort on the margin of Lough Foyle, below the Derry we have mentioned), and to take him prisoner. This was done, and he obtained the fort in his release. He repaired immediately at daybreak to Derry, and awoke the soldiers of that town with the sword. The Governor was slain by Owen, the son of Niall, son of Gerald O'Doherty, and Lieutenant Corbie by John, the son of Hugh, son of Hugh Duv O'Donnell. Many others were also slain besides these. Captain Henry Vaughan and the wife of the bishop of the town were taken prisoners. They afterwards plundered and burned the town, and carried away immense spoils from thence.

"Alas! although it was no wonder that this noble chieftain should have avenged his dishonour, innumerable and indescribable were the evils that sprang up and pullulated in the entire province of Ulster through this warlike rising, which he undertook against the King's law; for from it resulted his own death, on the 18th of July following, by the Chief Marshal of Ireland, Robert Wingfield, and Sir Oliver Lambert. He was cut into quarters between Derry and Cuil-mor, and his head was sent to Dublin, to be exhibited; and many of the gentlemen and chieftains of the province, too numerous to be particularized, were also put to death. It was indeed from it, and from the departure of the Earls we have mentioned, it came to pass that their principalities, their territories, their estates, their lands, their forts, their fortresses, their fruitful harbours, and their fishful bays, were taken from the Irish of the province of Ulster, and given in their presence to foreign tribes; and they were expelled and banished into other countries, where most of them died.

"Niall Garv O'Donnell, with his brothers Hugh Boy and Donnell, and his son, Naghtan, were taken prisoners about the festival of St. John in this year, after being accused of having been in confederacy with O'Doherty. They were afterwards sent to Dublin, from whence Niall and Naghtan were sent to London, and committed to the Tower, Niall having been freed from death by the decision of the law; and they Niall and Naghtan remained confined in the Tower to the end of their lives. Hugh and Donnell were liberated from their captivity afterwards, i.e. in the year following."

The Newsbooks

The three news reports on O'Doherty's Rebellion, *The Over-throw of an Irish rebell*, *Newes from Lough-foyle* and *Later Newes from Ireland* were sold in a small pamphlet format called a newsbook. The O'Doherty newsbooks are not considered to be newspapers because they are not serially numbered or dated as a periodical publication would be. When newspapers first appeared in London fifteen years later one of the first publishers was Nathaniel Butter, the publisher of *Newes from Lough-foyle* and *Later Newes from Ireland*. In 1608 Nathaniel Butter also published another booklet, the first edition of Shakespeare's *King Lear*. He should have stayed with the classics because his reputation suffered when he got into sensational journalism. Butter and his newspapers are satirized in Ben Johnson's play *The Staple of News*. The character Cymbal represents Nathaniel Butter and the word butter is worked into the script twenty times including some dialog about sour butter that was only suitable for suppositories and greasing wagon wheels. When his last newspaper went out of business a competitor reported "the greasie ghost of Nathaniel Butter spreading news about the world walks about in Print no more."

Newes from Lough-foyle is the first published of the three newsbooks. At the time of its publication O'Doherty was still alive and laying siege to Lifford. *Later Newes from Ireland* is an update of *Newes from Lough-foyle* which embellishes the details of Captain Hart's captivity and tells of the English forces that were enroute to the battle. *Newes from Lough-foyle* is included for completeness but it contains nothing in addition to *Later Newes from Ireland*.

The last of the three newsbooks to appear was *The Over-throw of an Irish rebell* sold by bookseller John Wright. Many titles were sold by Wright including the first printing of Shakespeare's *Sonnets*, Marlowe's *Doctor Faustus* and *Newes of Sir Walter Raleigh*. *The Over-throw of an Irish rebell* contains three parts: the news article, a *Letter from a Gentleman* in Ireland relating the events of the rebellion and a proclamation from the Lord Deputy of Ireland, Sir Arthur Chichester, announcing the death of O'Doherty and offering rewards for the capture or execution of his supporters. The proclamation was originally printed by John Franckton, a Dublin printer.

The woodcut illustration on the cover of *The Over-throw of an Irish rebell* shows two heads on poles over Newgate in Dublin. The second one is thought to be Phelim Reagh MacDavitt, one of O'Doherty's primary supporters. Newgate was a gate in the wall around the old city of Dublin. It is no longer standing but there are remnants of the old wall still visible at Lamb's Alley near Cornmarket.

The newsbooks have been electronically reset in type using 17th century replica fonts (JSL Ancient and JSL Blackletter) which are nearly identical to the originals. The ornaments, and ornate capitals are from the original newsbooks. Page layout has been preserved and spellings have not been changed. Some of the old typographic conventions which make the texts very difficult for the modern reader have been changed. For example the originals used a long letter "s" which was indistinguishable from an "f". Also, the letters "i" and "j" were frequently interchanged in the old texts as were "u" and "v". So "ivft cavfe" has been changed to "just cause". And "his maiefties" has been changed to "his majesties" but not to "his majesty's".

THE Ouer-throw of an Irish rebell, in a late battaile:

Or

The death of Sir *Carey Adoughertie*, who murdred Sir George Paulet *in Ireland*; and for his rebellion hath his head now standing ouer Newgate in Dublin.

Imprinted at London for I. Wright, and are to be sold at his shop neere Christ Church gate. 1608.

The overthrow of an
Irish Rebell.

Mongst all the diseases that infect the body of a kingdome, none is more dangerous then that mortall plague of Rebellion: It is a sicknesse not to bee cured but by letting bloud: And so much the more violently do the flames of these seditious fires burne, by how much the more gently with an easie breath, men seeke to put them out. Summon Traitors to friendly parlies, and they waxe proud, insolent, and fuller of mischiefe: there is no phisicke therefore for such desperate maladies in a State, but onely the sword; and it is most fit that they who lift up their arme against Gods annoynted, shold have their Traitorous and Rebellious heads layd bleeding at their soveraignes feete.

The country of Ireland hath (like a disobedient childe) runne from time to time into all lawlesse and Irreguler courses: pitty and piety have beene banished from her bosome: Justice hath had the sword snatched out of her hand to strike even those magistrats that were her faithfull ministers; order, ceremonies and religion have beene accompanied which cruelty, barbaous wildenesse and confusion, or rather not accompanied with them, but basely trodden down by by them: Yea to such a habit of Savage tirany hath Rebellion brought that nation, that nothing hath beene or still is pleasing to a great part of them, but that which all civill kingdomes abhor, (as beeing their onely plague) and that is Civill Warre: Murders and Massacres and uprores are to them as Musick & Banquets: bloud as the most delicate cups of wine: Thou needest not (O gallant country) to boast that no venemous beast is bread within thee, for the hearts of thy disobedient children are full of rancke poyson: Thou hast deserved to bee called not one of the daughters of *Britannia*, but to bee rejected as a bastard: and albeit from time to time, she hath beene unto thee as a loving Nurse and Mother, thou canst not condemne her of unkindenesse if shee prove unto thee a stepdame. How many hundreds of thousands of our English nation have beene drowned in their owne bloud, sluc'de out by thy treachery? how many of our Nobility have lost their lives and beene confounded, whilst in their duety and allegiance they went about to enduce thee to civility, or to chastize thee for thy Stubburnnes? how many widowes have bewailed the losse of their husbands, butcherd by thy rebellious people? how many sonnes and daughters by thy meanes have beene left fatherlesse? Yet if thou lookest backe (O *Ireland*) either upon the fortunate reigne of thy late Queene and mistresse

(of

of an Irish rebell,

(of happy memory) or doest but number up the daies of rest which thy now royall soveraigne (our most gracious King) hath in his peacefull and blessed government bestowed upon thee, thou canst not choose but confesse, that (thy ill deservings beeing so many) thou hast beene favorably dealt withall, in being not punished according to the measure of thy offendings: thou hast beene worthy to have beene beaten with rods of Iron for thy unrulinesse, and to have had fire the sword playe the executioners uppon thee and thy nation for their stiff-necked rebellion. But our Princes have beene unto thee in their correction as fathers are to children, when they punish them, yet nothing can win thee to goodnesse or weane thee from thy bloudy and barbarous proceedings.

But let us leave this streame, and hoist up sailes in the sea where our intent was at first to end our voiage. And that is to discover the onset and overthrow of a Rebell, or rather conductor of Rebells, Sir *Carey Adougherty*.

You shall therefore understand, that Sir *Carey Adoughertie*, having with his bloudie assiotiate (*Fallin Reeah Mack Davy*) committed that inhumaine murder upon Sir *George Paulet*, and others their inhabitantes of the towne of Derry, thought with the *Tragicall Poet Tutum, esse sceleribus per scelus itur*, that the onely buckler to defend villanies was to joyne the army of more

villanies

The overthrow

villanies to them: Being stepped up to the knees in bloud he perswaded himself that it was now no time to go back, but rather to wade on further, till hee came to the chimne: and carying about him a conscience guiltie not onely of murther, (a sinne that God never leaves unpunished) but also of his disloyaltie to his Soveraigne, in making uproares in his kingdomes, spoiling his subjects, and bringing his townes and citties (so farre as in his cruelty lay) to devastation; for which offence hee might worthily feare that the lawes of our land would call his life into question; his fortunes therefore, his honour, his life and loyalty (that was begunne to bee crackd) did hee set on a desperate case; and (with *Hherostratus*) resolved to bee famous albeit it were for nothing but in being a Traytor to his Prince and countrie, and in dooing mischiefe.

For which purpose, casting by all shame, all humanitie, all respect to his countrie and all regarde of that dutie, in which by reason of his place (as beeing chosen to bee one of the Aldermen of the towne of *Derry* he stood bound; Insteed thereof did hee arme his spirits with a setled ranckor against his Prince and his subjects; calling unto him a company of Irish whose hands did yet reeke with the bloud of the English most trecherously slaughtered and day by day increasing his rebellious multitude,
                                                       with

an Irish rebell.

with numbers of dissolute persons, that were apt to under-take any mischievous enterprize, men hardy enough to attempt, and resolute to execute, full of courage, if that courage had beene spent in honorable action; defying death, and any danger that could dant flesh and bloud, but yet so defying them, that it was rather out of a desperate fortune, then any constant fortitude, or noble valour.

This nest of Serpents, being thus hatched in mischiefe, were quickly fledged and being fethered with ambition, treason, insurrection, and tyrannie, the body of them grew to bignesse, and in a short time, from a handfull, did their numbers increase, til they were nine hundred strong or eleven hundred at the most.

Then did this Ring-leader of Rebels wax insolent and haughtie: Fortunes nette he thought was put into his hands, and the draught which he made was to pull up a kingdome: but the tree of Rebellion spreds fairely and largely at first, it promiseth great store of fruite, but so many Cater-pillers hang upon it, and so rotten it is at the heart, that it withereth faster then it groweth, and is hewne downe and destroyed by the weight of his owne branches that fall upon it. How can a petty River contend with the maine Ocean? how can a Candle dim the glory of the Sunne? And what madnesse is it then for a meane subject to wrastle against the royall authority

The over-throw,

thoritie of his Soveraigne? Yet did Sir *Carey Adoughertie* in the heigth of his prowd over-weening, thinke that like a whirle-winde hee should throw downe all that with-stood his furie, and that like a storme at Sea, the whole kingdome of Ireland should vaile to him, to save it selfe from shipwrack. But God, whose Angels, are the garde of Princes persons, and whose right hand steeres the helme, by which Kingdomes are governed, did arme the Lord Deputie, and the Councell of Ireland, not one-lie with present courage to encounter this Re-bell, but with wisedome to prevent, and to beat backe all stormes that by his boysterous and and turbulent spirits were threatned to disquiet the peaceable state of the country.

One thousand English are therefore forth-with levied, and those divided into three regiments, under the conducts of these Gentlemen and others, viz

Sir *Thomas Ridgeway,* Treasurer for Ireland.

Sir *Richard Wingfield,* Knight Marshall of Ireland

Sir *Oliver Lambert.*
Sir *Richard Morrison.*
Sir *Thomas Roper.*
Sir *Francis Rush.*
Sir *Toby Cofeild.*
Sir *Josias Bodley.*

And

And besides these, diverse gentlemen of name, all of them, using their best pollicie, to cut off the forces of the enemy: And because, they would bee sure, that hee should not escape out of the nettes prepared for him, those three thousand so divided into three severall companies were directed to march three severall waies into the countrie, and by that meanes the Rebell, if hee durst come into the fielde, might bee encompassed and set upon.

Before I proceede any further, it shall not bee amisse to set downe one matter, as an argument, to expresse the confidence that Sir *Cary Adoughertie* had in his forces, as also to shew the pride and highnesse of his spirit, and that was thus.

The Bishoppe of Derry and of those parts of the country had his wife surprized by Sir Carry & his accomplices, and by them held prisoner: no intreaty of the bishop, no nor the ransome of a thousand pound (which hee offred) could buy her out of their hands: whereupon the bishop (who freely passed too & fro, aswel to Sir *Cary* as to the English that were his friends, without disturbance, because he was a church-man) entred into speech with the rebell, about his unnaturall proceedings against the peace of his country. But *Adougherty* being careles of his reprehension, in the end spake thus. I understand (quoth he)

that

The over-throw,

that your Hotte-spur of the East (meaning Sir *Thomas Ridgeway,* the Treasurer) purposes to come into the field against me: I doe not thinke (sayes Sir *Carey*) he dare venture so farre, because hee's riche: But tell him insteed of his gold and silver, I will meete him with a good strong sword; hee shall have sundry messes at his table, and be as well served as ever hee was in his life, and to tell him.

But (for all these braves of the rebell,) Sir *Thomas Ridgeway* came into the field and shewed his loyaltie to his Prince, and love to his country by his excellent service, performed by him that day, when the fight was.

The streame of civill sedition, like a Land-torrent, the higher it swels, the more unresistable it is: order therefore was suddainely taken, to meete with these rebellious troopes, so soone as possibly they could, to hinder the joyning of more forces to them. And whereas a fresh supply was sent over from England of soldiers, that were but raw & unexperienced in the wars; those bands were kept about Dublyn, and the old tryed soldiers were drawne forth, and appointed to undertake this businesse.

About the middle of June last, did they come into the field (being as I said before three thousand onely, and divided into three companies.) The place where this worke of death was to be finished, was within ten or twelve miles of the

Derry,

Derry, an equall desire there was both in the English and the Irish to encounter and meete one another: and albeit the English had the advantage of men, besides the uprightnesse of the quarrell, yet were the Irish nothing daunted; or terrified with multitude; but being full of hope, and desperately valiant, bravely kept together. The Musicke of warre struck upon both sides, to give encouragement to those that wanted no Spurres to prick them forward. Bravely was the onset given, and as bravely answered: you would have thought that Thunder had beene onely upon earth, the Gunnes did speake so lowd and with such dreadfull voices: yea swords meeting with swords, threw abroad such sparkles of fire, that the field seemed to bee all made of flames, and that the *Ætnæan* fornace had there beene kindled. Armes and legges flew up into the ayre, to mock the aspiring ambition of them that wore them, who ventured the losse of their owne blouds, to trouble the still waters of a peacefull kingdome; whilst their sencelesse heads lay weeping on the ground for the folly of their maisters that could no better keepe them.

   The end of all battailes is to have conquest on the one side or the other: but Fortune holding the Dice of warre in her hand, made them run so equally, that it was hard to know which side should winne the victory. Many houres they

they fought with answerable courage, and answerable fortune; till at length, one of those three companies, into which the English troopes were divided, secretly keeping aloofe, came up on the suddaine and unexpected of the enemy, on the back of the Rebell, so that hee was rouudly beset with death and his officers. They were like a heard of lustie Deere encompassed with huntsmen, and every minute looked to heare the knell of their deaths rung forth, yet to shew that albeit they scorned life, they would not give it away for nothing, they fought couragiouslie, because they purposed to sell their bloud deerely. But (alas!) what strength of man can hold out when the finger of God is held up against them? God added vigor, and knitte the sinews of the loyall Subject, that hee might bee of power to confound the trayterous rebell. And that their pride might bee confounded even in that person, that first made them faithlesse to their countrie, and foes to their Soveraigne: heaven opened the hand of divine vengeance, and from it shotte a bullet, which strooke Sir *Carey Adoughertie* quite through the head. The wound was mortall, for with it, hee presently fell downe and dyed; and so fell downe, that his hand laye directly under his cheeke, (his head leaning upon it) and so was found slaine about some three houres after hee was shotte; the head beeing
after

afterwards cut off from the shoulders by one of Sir *Francis Rush* his men, And from the field sent to Dublin, where it standeth (fixed on a pole,) over the East-gate of the citty, called New-gate.

In this skirmish were lost on the English side very few; of the Irish many; for the leader being cut off, those that were his followers in so dishonest and dishonorable an action, fainted, and felt the deserved justice of the warres, so that in a short time, they were all either slaine or (as chaff by a furious winde) blowne away & dispersed to nothing. Since which defeat diverse of the Rebels are come in of their owne accord, and daily more and more doe submit themselves to that mercy, which Sir *Arthur Chichester* (the Lord deputy) hath by proclamation offred unto them.

Thus have I set downe the over-throwe of a man, whose fortunes might have bin better, had not a turbulent & revenging spirit dwelt in his bosome: But as the course of his life was bloudy, so (by the just doome of heaven) was the conclusion of it. God never suffers a hand that takes a pride to be embrewed in slaughter, to scape unpunished. Note the ends of all such mutinous and barbarous-minded Rebels, that have burnt up their country with the fires of civill uproares, and have layd wast the hopes of the poore hus-bandman, and you shall see that their deathes have beene as suddaine, as bloudy,
and

The over-throw

and as desperate, as their lives were treacherous, and seditious: let the fall therefore of this Rebell, bee a warning to all other his countrymen, that they revolt not from that naturall love and allegiance, which they are bound in conscience, in religion, and by the lawes of the kingdome to pay unto their Prince and Soveraigne, least the selfe-same or a worse confusion follow not onely them in the heigth of their traiterous enterprizes, but their children and posteritie to be eraced for ever from the face of the earth.

A Let-

A Letter from a Gentleman

out of Ireland, confirming not onely the trueth
of the late report touching the newes of Lough-
foyle, but also this last action wherein
O Doughertie was slaine.

Orthy friend, what you may see, and assure yourselfe, that the sea hath not washt away my old love, nor this remote place remooved my affection from that which it once it was, I write these lines, having heretofore acquainted you with my stedfast- nesse in that kinde by a former letter. And because this can be but an idle repetition of that especially if you beleeve mee to bee honest harted towards you, and a professor onely of what I thinke. I will omitte all complements, and plainly say that I love you truly, and that for the greatnesse of the worth that I have found in you, which if you beleeve 'tis enough, if not all I can say will be too little; and so much for that. Now to our newes; take it as it is, though at the se- cond hand, and perhaps knowne before.

I assure myselfe you have heard of the sudainesse of O Doghorties action, and the burning of the Derry long since: and therefore to let that passe, I will follow him briefely in his other actions, till I have pursued him to his death. Thus then.

After the rumor of this report was certainely
knowne,

A Letter.

knowne, such forces as Ireland then had of the kings, were with some indifferent expedition made ready, and committed to the leading of the *Marshall* Sir Richard Winckfield, and Sir Oliver Lambert, the whole number amounting to 600 or there about. who passing to the Derrie without hearing of the rebell, made from thence to Culmore, a Forte some foure mile from it, which he had taken from Captaine Harry Hart by treacherie before, which was quit by those that kept it for the rebel, before our forces could sit downe before it, so that it was got with as much ease as lost, though more honorably: for O Doghertie being Captaine Harts gossip, had under colour of friendship invited him and his wife to his house (as he had often done before) and having him there, kept him prisoner, and swore to his wife unlesse she would use some meanes to deceive the warders, and deliver him the Castle, her husbands life should answer for it, which to save she performed the night before the Derry was burnt. This Castle our forces having againe gotten, they marched after him, to fight with him if he would endure, where they understood hee was: but hee having no such purpose, quit his owne country, and went into Mack Swines, being a place of more fastnesse. His wife, sister & daughter he had left in his country in a strong castle of his owne, whither after his flight our forces kept their course, and having summond it, & receav'd a peremptory answer from the Constable thereof, they brought a peece of Ordinance before it, from which the shot being made, & an offer of an assault given, did so daunt the defendants,

A Letter.

dants, that they yeelded both the castle and companie in it to the *Kings* mercy, where the *Bishop of* Derry (a most valiant & worthy *Prelate*) recovered his wife so long deteined by the rebels, and for whose ransome he had a few dayes before proferd 500 pound, which was refused. O Dogherties *Lady*, sister & daughter being an infant, were with some others sent to the *Castle of* Dublin where they yet remaine. *After this blow given him, his Kernes seeing their hope perish, earnestly prest him to do somthing against the kings forces, or there vowd to leave him, which he undertooke to do. This being concluded, they appointed to set upon our men at the edge of a wood, as they should passe (going then to besiege Doe castle which he held) & there to cut off some of our forces. But notice being given, they found a hote welcome. When* O Dogherty (*having valor fitting a better man*) *thought to doe somthing worthy himselfe, and therefore caused his foster father* Phelim Reugh *to lead a wing of shot, and himselfe came up in the reare, which was well performed, but in the going off, he being somthing to busie in shaking his Pike in a vaine florish, was by a soldier of Sir* Francis Rush *his company noted (though not for him) and shotte through the head:* Phelim Reuhg *seeing him fall, wheeled back and bestrid the body, thinking to recover it, which made the soldier gesse him to be a man of speciall note that was slaine, and therefore (being not so sodainly able to charge his Peece againe) hee put powder into his panne, and made a false proffer, which* Reugh *perceiving, and fearing the like fortune, left the body and fledde, uppon which accident our men advanced forward,*
and

A Letter.

and gaind his body: and this was his end who did so ill begin, and layd the foundation of his rebellion in the bloud of his neighbor. Thus having hunted him to his death which hath beene a tedious track, I will not dare to undertake a fresh sport in this kinde, though there are many Foxes in this kingdome. But for Tyrone, and Tyreconnell, they are already fled from their covect, and I hope will never returne; and for other of false hartes the cheefe of note, as O Cave, Sir Neale O Donnell, alias, Neale Garve, and his two brothers, with others of their condition, have hoales provided for them in the Castle of Dublin, where I hope the are safe enough for breeding any Cubbs to disquiet or prey upon the flock of honest subjects in this kingdome.

BY

BY THE LORD DEPUTIE and Councell.

Arthure Chichester.

Whereas it hath pleased Almighty God so to blesse his Majesties Armie, in pursuit of that wicked Rebell O-Doghertie, and his Adherents, as that on Tuesday last, being the fifth of this said Moneth of July, the said O Doghertie, was happily slaine, neere a place called Kilmacrenan, in the Countie of Tirconnell: Wherein God hath not onely shewed his just judgement upon this treacherous Creature, but doth plainely declare to this Nation, and to all the World, that shame and confusion is the certaine & infallible end of all the Traytors and Rebels,

We have therefore thought fit, not onely to notifie and publish the killing of the said Traytor, to all his Majesties good and loyall Subjects, but also in regard to Adherents and followers of the said O Dogherty, in his late Rebellion, are now broken and scattered, and are like to put themselves and theyr goodes under the wing and protection of such as have continued in their obedience: We do hereby fore-warne all good subjects, that

A Proclamation.

that none of them do presume to relieve, entertaine, receive, or protect any person or persons whatsoever, who hath beene Actors, Councellors, and followers of the said O Doghertie in his late Action of rebellion, upon paine to bee reputed and adjudged traitors in as high a degree as the sayd O Doghertie himselfe, or any his Adherents. Notwithstanding We doe promise, that whosoever shall deliver or bring unto us the Lord Deputy, or any his Majesties principall Commanders or Officers of his Armie; the body or bodies of any person or persons, dead or alive, who have been followers of the said O Doghertie in his sayd rebellion; beeing Sword-men or Owners of Goods or Creathes, shall have for his reward, not onely his Majesties gratious pardon, but also all the goods of such person or persons whom hee shall so deliver or bring unto us (Phelim Reough mac David, and Shane mac Manus oge onely excepted) who must expect no pardon, but whosoever shall bring the said Phelims head, or deliver his body alive, shall have the full benefit of our former Proclamation in that behalfe.

Given at Dundalke the bii of July, 1608.

God save the King.

Thomas Dublin Cane.   Thom. Ridgeway.
       H. Winche.   Oliver St. John.
Henry Harrington.   Geff. Fenton.
Richard Morrison.   H. Power.
Adam Loftus.   Rich. Cooke.

DUBLIN
Printed by John Franckton, Printer to the
Kings most excellent Majestie.
1608.

LATER
Newes from
Ireland.

Concerning the late *treacherous*
Action, and rebellion, of Sir Carey *Adoug-*
hertie, and Felli Me Reeah Mack
Davy.

With the cunning & deceitefull surprising
of *Captaine* Hart, *his wife and Children,* and
the Castle of Kilmore, his ransacking &
burning of the Cittie of
Derry &c.

And the inhumane murther of Sir George Paulet, his associates, and most of the inhabitants
of the Derry aforesaid.

Newly imprinted and inlarged by further
instructions.

LONDON
Printed for Nathaniell Butter, and are to be
solde at his shop in Paules Church-yard,
neere Saint Austens Gate
1608

NEWES
From Ireland, out of Lough-foyle:

Concerning the late treacherous Action;
and rebellion of Sir Carey Adougherty, *and*
Felli Me Reeah Mack Davie, as first, the cunning and deceitful surprising of Captaine
Hart his wife and Children, with
the Castle of *Kilmore.*

S in the naturall bo-
dy of man there is no
forme or constitution
so excellent and perfit,
but hath in it some taste
of corrupt humors to
disturbe and deface the
workmanship of nature,
So in the politick body
of a Kingdome or Common-wealth, there is
no governments, though never so well managed and setled, but hath still bred in it some corrupt Male-contents, and Maligners of the state:

nor

Newes from Ireland

nor that any countrie is so subject thereunto as that of Ireland appeares by recordes left from former ages, which the condition of the present times confirme.

The happie Raign of the late deceased Queen of famous memorie, How was it not onely traduced by the calumnious tongues of Catholickes, & all the popish crew, But her life also so often endangered, that not a yeare past without some notable and divelish plot and project, which neverthelesse by God his especial power & grace, did still faile in the execution: but above all, that hellish & abhorred Treason, which in the third yeare of his Majesties raigne, was so cunningly and daungerously contrived, both against the head and principall members of the Kingdome, did so farre excell all comparison, that unto strange nations the reporte thereof hath yet scarse entred the compasse of beleefe: the effecting whereof had prepared miserie for the childe unborne.

Oh that the wombe of a Country should beare such prodigious monsters, and that the aire of any Climate should give them breath, that like the Earth-born brethren, envying each others shape, devours another! For the unquiet minde of man never content with his owne estate, doth passe through all sortes of opinions and purposes, untill she hath setled the ground of her device, which if

it

Newes from Ireland

it be framed in the webbe of mischiefe, oh what a work doth it produce, so contrary to the quiet nature of man, that no single eye or wel disposed heart but doth abhor it? This discontentment of minde or rather unreasonable & ambitious dersire of glory, is a vice that seduceth the hearts of many subjects from their loyall & duetifull obedience, & fights against modesty, which is a part of temperance. For the modest man (as *Aristotle* saith) desireth honor, as he ought, & as becommeth him. but he that desireth it by unlawful meanes, is ambitious, & caried away with a perturbation of intemperance. Of such as these, there are many examples, both in sacred and prophane Histories, which may instruct and warn loyall subjects: Amongst whome commeth here to my remembrance, the notable storie of *Korah* that seditious headed, & ambitious minded Israelite whose rebellion on *Moses* at large setteth downe with his bad successe and strange punishment. In which ambition (as commonlye it falleth out with men infected with that vice) there was first mal-contentment of minde, who not satisfied with that honor & calling wherin he was placed, raised up disquietnes & disturbance among the people. Secondly, there was in him an envious affection, wherby he disdained that *Moses* & *Aaron* should have any power over him. Thirdly, like our vile Anabaptists, he went about to suppres government, & wold have all to be

of

Newes from Ireland

of equall power and condition, which is the confusion of all estates of people. Fourthly, he raised up open sedition & Rebellion against Governors appointed of God. Fiftly, he went about to have brought the high Priest-hood, from *Aron* unto himselfe, although he found fault with others for the same. The holy Scriptures are full of examples, both of Ambitious proceedings, and of the deserved fall and ruine of such unnaturall and undutiful intendments: so likewise are prophane histories.

As what but Ambition stird up *Cæsar* and *Pompey*, *Marius* & *Scilla*, *Octavius*, *Antonius*, & *Lepidus*, by force of armes to put their Country to Sword and fire, and so unnaturally to impaire the large & great scope of the Romaine Empire? What but ambition & discontentment of mind hath drawne many desperate people from time to time, not onelye to cast out words of disdaine against the honorable rule and reverence of the higher powers, but to forsake their loyall and bounden dueties, and (without any compunction of conscience) to practise the subversion of King, commonwealth and Countrie.

I neede not enlarge myself in this matter, either by divine or prophane examples: our home-bred experience and testimonie, may serve from time to time to expresse the follyes of such ambitious persons, as have beene led either by envie or presumpti-

out of Lough-foyle

sumption, to lift up hand against their head, and so worke their owne falles and destructions. To set aside the Treasonable practises of discontented Papists, & other malevolent opposites to the State, Many other commotions and insurrections of the giddie-headed and ungoverned people, uppon false and fained pretexts and suggestions, having alwaies bene without ground in the foundation, have likewise bene without forme in the building: So dissonant to the well tuned peace & tranquility of the Land, that many times it hath mard that goodly consent and harmony, wherewith both heaven and earth is delighted. Such was the rebellion of *Jack Straw* and *Wat Tyler* in the daies of Richard the second, at that time when in his minoritie, hee gat a singuler hope and expectation of a happie raigne & government. The like in the time of *Henry* the sixt, by *Jack Cade*, that assumed the name of *Mortimer* in the disturbance of the peaceable condition of his Raigne, which though it had a ground and project, plotted by the Duke of *Yorke*, that then made a claime and title to the Crowne, and happily from him a countenance assisting therunto, yet were the proceedings mishapen, & the successe answerable.

Kets commotion in Norfolk in the raigne of *Edward* the sixt, a moste excellent Prince, being without just cause, or colour either of their own greevances, or the Kings government, did in a short time
growe

Newes from Ireland

growe to such a body, but so horrid & monstrous, that at this day there are misshapen monuments left of that prodigious Rebellion. The rebellyon of *Tyrone* in *Ireland*, in the daies of her late majesties happie raigne, how monstrous was it in respect of the mischiefes it brought with it, and left behinde it? How unnaturall in respect of the many miseries and untimely deathes that it wrought, even to his owne Countriemen? how unthankfull in respect of the manifolde favours hee reeceived at the handes of his Soveraigne, to whome hee worthily owed his deerest blood, his life, and all that ever he enjoyed?

But the endes of all such as have practised Rebellion, who is so ignorant that he hath not either read or heard them, or so voide of understanding that he cannot prejudicate of their successe? and fith in this case there is occasion present ministred to write (though I could be content my penne were rather idle then busied in the treatye of such a subject) I have thought good, so farre as my instructions lead me, to make knowne to the world the nature and manner of the late most cruell and unnatural proceedings of some of *Tyrone* his accomplices in *Ireland*, upon the bodyes of divers of his Majesties faithfull and loving Subjects. in setting downe of which infamous Actes and attempts of murther & treason, I shall labour to exhort all well disposed
Subjects,

Newes from Ireland.

Subjects to the duetie of obedience, and exhort al factious & turbulent spirits from the treasonable & ill relisht poyson of Rebellion, that being once distasted in the pallate of conceit, it may hereafter not infect the heart with consent: And I do much wonder that reasonable men should in this case bee much worse then insensible creatures: the one still naturally striving to preserve, and the other unnaturally to destroy their kinde: and if they would but rightly examin the qualitie and condition of times past, together with the nature of murther, Treason, and rebellions, they should soone finde that as the successe hath failed them in their expectations, so their punishments have still suted to their deservings, & that justly too, for where offence is but tollerated by authoritie, or incouraged by impunitie, There insolencie and mens misbehaviours commaund the law, which is the greatest error (I suppose) that can be in government.

So preposterous and out of order are the devices and attempts of Rebellion and treacherie, that such as are misled by their directions, doe never measure their owne actions by time, or their affections by discretion, but in a head-strong & improvident course, undertake & prosecute their rash & heedeles enterprises, oftentimes to the ruine & destruction of themselves & many others. But above all, this late cruell and bloudy plot, practiced about *Loughfoyle* in *Ireland* as it ought with all pietie to be pittied, so deserves it to bee remembred, as a demonstrance of the Irish inhumantie: who notwithstanding his majesties lenitie & many gratious favours towards them, have stil continued their wilfull and bloudie courses, without and just cause or ground, what colour soever they set upon it, to face the garment of their rebellion, their hearts being so obdurate & inclined to mischiefe, that they quite forget to understand how unlawfull & undutifull

thei

Newes from Ireland.

their actions are, how offensive to God and to the King, aswell in the duties of devotion as obedience: how hurtfull in regard of example to others, how hopelesse in regard of successe to themselves, how dangerous in respect of their states present, and how infamous in the consideration of times to come: when (notwithstanding the best glosse & colour they can set upon their attempts) they shal yet in after times (as others have done in former) carry the verye names & faces of Traitors, and march in the hated rankes of *Jacke Straw*, *Wat Tyler*, *Jacke Cade* and others, being marked with the odious and detestable brand and stampe of Rebels.

This *Lough-foyle* is a River in the North part of *Ireland*, bounded on the one side with the countrie of *Ocane* and *Tyrone*, and on the other, with the Lands and living of *Oddonnell* and of Sir *Carey Adougherty*, a Rebell by whome this late murther and Treacherie was chieflie plotted and prosecuted: It is adjoyning to the Ilands betweene *Scotland* & *Ireland*, and about some eight yeares since or somewhat more in the time of the great rebellion, this place was surprised and taken by the worthy knight Sir *Henry Dockwray*, whose first landing was at *Kilmore*, about twelve miles of the right hand of the River within the Country, and the then country of Sir *John Adoughertie* (father of this Sir *Carey*, who was at that time living. Here Sir *Henrie Dockwray*, founded a Castle against the River aforesaid, which he very sufficiently fortified, & afterwards made a strong Forte there called *Kilmore*. Within one moneth following, he went three miles beyond that, and tooke the *Derry* without any resistance, lying upon the said River of *Loughfoyle*, where is since erected a goodly Town called the Citie of the *Derry*, and where also he built two Fortes, and a goodly house.

After this, he made another Forte called *Dun a Longe* a
place

Newes from Ireland.

place some three miles beyond that, on the left hand of the River, and then the *Leffierd* some twelve miles beyond the *Derrie*.

But changes and alterations are (for the most part) full of perills and daunger, and the mischaunces doe soonest befall us, when we account our selves most secure, and are best perswaded of our safety: as hapned to Sir *George Paulet* of Hampshier, who went into *Ireland* with his wife and children, and was made Governour of the *Derry* aforesaid, by the assignement of Sir *Henry Dockewray*, the which place Sir Henry had formerly obtained in the time of war, by his owne valour and industry.

But to satisfie the Readers expectations of the trecherous attempts of Sir *Cary Adougherty* aforesaid, which is the onely purpose of this present relation, you shall understand, that as the Serpent never stings more deadly, then when hee bites without hissing, so an enimie never intends more deep mischeife and villany, then when he shaddowes his purposes under the shew & pretext of friendship and amitie.

In what bloody manner dealt *Joab* with *Abner*? when he pretended to speak peaceably with him in the gate? concerning which trecherous manner, *David* left order with *Salomon* his sonne, to which *Salomon* agreed and caused *Benaiah* to smite *Joab*, having caught holde on the hornes of the Altar, and there hee died.

In what trecherous manner have many hipocrites made Feasts, and in the middest of their cuppes imbrued their hands with blood? To omit the butchery of *Abimilech*, uppon his brethren, for the placing himselfe in the Kingdome: to omit the poisoning of King *John*, King of *England* by a Moncke of Swinsthead Abbey: the murther fresh in memory, done by a Frier most bouldly upon *Henry* the late King

Newes from Ireland.

King of *France*: the villanous attempt upon the Prince of *Orrenge*: To passe over the abhominable crueltie of the *Guizians*, bathing themselves in blood in the time of the massacre and that practise against the Lord *Chastillon*, the Lord high Admirall of *France*, And to omit to speak of *Bothwel* his villany, not any way inferiour, or behinde the rest in savage crueltie: for his treason against our King his most excellent majestie: this un-heard of manner of treacherie, contrived and effected by Sir *Cary Adougherty*, is, for the exercise as monstrous, & for the execution, as cruell & tiranous as any that is or can be mentioned.

He made shew and protestation of great love and friendship he beare to Captaine *Hart*, who was left commaunder of the Forte and Castle of Kill-more, but under the cloake and habit of amity, he shrowded the hate and heart of an enemie. *Simulata æquitas, non est æquitas, sed duplex iniquitas, quia iniquitas est & simulatio*: fained equitie is no equitie but a double iniquitie, because it is iniquitie and dissimulation: Such a one hath this Irishe rebell shewed himselfe. *Intus Nero, foris Cato*: In shew, grave as *Cato*, and friendly as a Senatour: in heart as cruell as *Nero*, and as tirannous as a thirstie blood-sucker: As a beast compact of many beastes, According to the Poets saying, *Leo pars prima, Draco media Ipsa Chimera*: The principall and fore-part a Lyon, the middle part a Dragon, a very Chymera it selfe: Such a one is he as *Salomon* speaketh of, that invites a man to his table in shew of curtesye, and meanes him mischeife, that offers himselfe in renewing of friendship to eate and drink with a man, and as though he said in his heart, eate and drinke, but his heart is not with thee.

Such a one was *Judas*, who accompaining Christ as his Disciple, eating and drinking with him, did yet with a *Judas* kisse

Newes from Ireland.

kisse betray him: and such a one (I say) is this rebel Sir *Carey Adougherty*: he made great shew of love to Captaine *Hart*, but it was not with his heart, for he harboured an inward & secret rancour and malice, wherof he meant ere long to give open signe and outward demonstration, as it thus hapned.

 This Sir *Carey Adougherty* being so well thought on that hee was graced with dignitie of Knight-hood, made Alderman of the Cittie of *Derry*, and joyned in commission with other Justices of the Peace in those parts of Ireland: The 18 of Aprill last, invited Captaine Hart to dinner with his wife and little Sonne, and feasted them verie long, and that in such costly and sumptuous manner, as their extraordinarie and kinde entertainment for the present, & the long under-hand love that hee formerly pretended to shew to the Captaine, did quite remoove all feare and suspition of any treachery to follow.

 There was such familiarity betweene Captaine Hart and this Sir *Carey Adougherty*, is not long before sir *Carey* became his Gossip, and christned the Captaine a little Sonne, & not twelve monethes before that, Captaine *Hart* purchased of him three thousand Acres of ground, lying not far from his Castle, which he purposed to inhabit with English, and to that intent had written many letters to his friendes in Engand to furnish him with Tennants to take the same land of him. Besides all this, such was the estimation of his integritie both towards Prince and Countrie, that those partes where he inhabited being knowne to be savage and barbarous, & the people verie rude and irreguler, he was thought worthy not above a fortnight before the lamentable & treacherous surprising of the castle of Kilmore, & the cittie of Derry, to meet at the *Lefferd* with Sir *Richard Hinsard*, captaine *Hart*, Captaine *Vaughan*, and other Commissioners, about reformation

Newes from Ireland

mation of the abuses of that Countrey: and the establishing of certaine rules concerning the affaires, and service of his Majestie, whereof they had lately before receaved directions from the Lord Deputy: As namely the electing and swearing of Constables, the suppressing of certaine wilde Wood-karnes (which this Rebell complained his owne Tenants did harbour) and the appeasing of a controversie betweene two neighbours, that did arise by the fiering of an house nere Sir *Carey*, and within his Countrie.

These intercourses of busines and contractes of other friendships and amitie, were free from the least doubt and surmise of any treacherie: But he that alwaies carried in his heart an inward and secret infection of malice and envie, intended also that his action should give instance thereof against Captaine *Harts* securitie: For dinner being done, (to which Captaine *Hart* was so solemnly invited) and the time so farre over past, that the approach of night summoned him and his companie home to his charge, Captain *Hart* beginning to take his leave, and to give hearty thankes for the entertainement hee had received *Adougherty* changed the coppie of his countenance, and (calling him aside, pretending to speake a worde or two with him in private) told him, that this was but a traine to intrappe him, and a faire and sweete beginning, to drawe on a foule and sharpe conclusion, That he had received many disgraces from the English, and especially from Sir *George Pawlet* governour of the *Derry*, wherof he meant ere long to be revenged: Which words were no sooner uttered, but certaine armed men (placed before to that purpose) did presently rush in, disarmed Captaine *Hart*, and tooke him prisoner: And told him that if hee would not deliver

Newes from Ireland

liver up the Castle of Kilmore, he should see his wife and little childe kild before his face, and him selfe and such as were in the Castle, should pay the price of his deniall, even with their deerest bloodes.

Captaine *Hart* was nothing daunted or discouraged at this sodaine alteration, or with this Rebelles threats and menacings, but was armed with a loyall resolution, to abide any tyrannous crueltie that hee could inflict upon him: Preferring his owne honesty, and the duty hee owed to his Soveraigne, and to the welfare of his Country, before the life either of himselfe, his wife or children, or any other private respects: defiing the Rebell and his threats to his face, and chosing rather to die then to yeeld to such a villany: whereupon *Adoughertie* wild him to resolve to dye and so left him to the custody of those armed men.

To what extremitie and amazement may wee thinke this Captaine driven to, when (being thus left) on the one side he might behold so many sterne countenances to affright him? on the other such rough intreaties to terrifie him? and every way such imminent and open arguments of danger to destroie hin? who notwithstanding, even as a wise ship-maister, when hee setteth forth from the shoare and goeth to Sea, laieth a side the remembrance of wife and children, house and familye, and imployeth his body and minde only to the due performance of his duty, Soe Captaine *Hart*, being but newly lanched out of the porte of delicate faire and contentntement (as he was a guest) into a sodaine Sea and tempest of daunger & discomfort (as he was taken prisoner) did yet so displaye the saile of his love and loyaltie uppon the mast of his countries cause, that he betook himself wholy to the tackling of resolution, & kept his heart upon the sterne of due obedience

to

Newes from Ireland

to his Soveraigne, and rather desired to bee in the hand of danger, then to hazard the report of his name to any future imputation.

 Our heavenly Smith, suffered his allegiance to be broght into the forge of tryal and the coales of treacherous proceedings to be kindled, to proove whether he were pure golde and fit to be laid up in his princes treasurie: For many are judged by their shewes to be equall and obedient, whome tryall proveth of unequall and turbulent dispositions. Many flowers promise a multitude of fruit, but when they are once put to the proofe by stormes of winde, very few persever to the full growth. Pray God there be many, (that seeming faithfull in the calme and fruit of their content) will not bee found in the laps of disloyaltie, if the like blasts of Tryall & temptation doe bluster against them. This windie storme of treacherie, did for the space of two houres (for so long hee continued in the custodie of those armed men) continually assay to blow his loialty away like light chaff, & yet it resisted to the blastes like massy wheate: neyther faire nor foule meanes could draw him from the love & fayth that he owed to his Soveraigne, But after those two houres were past, the said Sir *Carey* A*doughertie*, returning to him againe, found him stil resolute in the denyal of the castle of *Kilmore*, which was the marke this Rebell aymed at, to inforce him to surrender. He indeavoured by all flights and violence to overcome him, but God armed him with truth against his encounters, he planted his batterie, and used all possible engines to overthrowe the rampyre and bulwark of his resolution, But all was in vaine: his force was too feeble, and his Engines to weake to batter downe the Adamant rock of his love and loyaltie, to his King and countrie, and therefore did but spurne against a thorne. Which Sir *Carey* perceiving,
willed

Newes from Ireland

willed the said armed men to doe execution uppon him: But where man bends his wicked courses to spill and destroy, God useth his secret power and povidence to save and preserve.

For Captaine *Hartes* wife marveiling at the long absence of her husband, (who was thus detained by force) in the meane time pressed into the chamber where he was, and finding his cause to hange in such a desperate suspence, betweene life and death, she fell downe in such a dangerous sowne, that she was taken up by *Adoughertyes* own wife, being almost past hope of recovery. The wife of this Rebell being an eye witnesse of her husbands trecherous proceedings: & being toucht with an inward feeling & compassion of the distresse & danger of these enthralled persons, could not but burst into teares, & make outward show of her inward sorrow for them: And perceiving the foulenes of the fact, how odious it was in respect of their obedience, and how trecherous in regard of that shewe of freindship (which this Rebell did alwaies pretend to beare to this Captaine) shee did utterly renounce, and disclaime to have any parte or privity of her husbands intent.

Sir *Carey Adoughertye* perceiving this, and seeing that all his former attempts upon the person of Captaine *Hart* would not prevaile to attaine his purpose, or to worke his disloyalty, thrust both his owne wife and the Captaine downe the staires, (yet so as hee confined him to the custody of certaine armed men in another place) and kept his wife backe, meaning to deale with her, as a more weake and easie instrument to bee wrought uppon, to bring to passe what hee shot att.

Her hee threaned with many othes and protestations, that if she did not yeelde her consent and furtherance to deli-

ver

Newes from Ireland

render unto his possesion the Castle of Kilmore, hee wold presently hang her husband, murther her little Sonne (that he christned) and then kill her. She (like a paper wall that breakes with one knock) not used before to such rough & savadge manner of intreatie, had not power to withstand him, especially seeing so great danger to be set before his eies as also perceiving the rebels fury to bee implacable, but yelded to his treacherous demaund: And so in the night hee carried her to the Castle, and caused her to call to her Servants to open the Castle gates, saying (being inforced thereunto) that her husband had broken his arme by a casuall, & disaster accident.

As soone as the gates were open, the Rebels entred, and possessed themselves of the castle, & presently being armed, went up with Captain Harts wife into the chamber of her eldest brother, being a knights sonne and heire of good account in England, who was but latelye come thither to see his Sister.

The young Gentleman was agast at the appearance of so many armed men in his bed-chamber, and began to bestirre himselfe. But his Sister soone crid out to him (being in bed) that he should not move nor stand in his defence, for if hee did, hee were but a dead man. Heere these Rebels made havocke of what they could finde: and tooke away al Captain Harts plate, stocke, and goods whatsoever, to a great value, and his utter undooing for ever.

And when they had done their violence and outrage at their pleasure (being by estimation three hundreth) leaving sufficient force to keepe the Castle in their behalfe, they departed from thence, to the prosecuring of further mischiefe and treacherie.

This strooke colde to the Captaines heart, yet at first hee

Newes from Ireland.

hee thought it but a fourme of feare put uppon him in jest, but when hee perceived by the continuance both of this Rebell, his sterne behaviour and countenance, and by the violent rushing in of those armed men, that it was past jest, and a purpose, practised in good earnest.

Seeing no other remedie, he began to fall to intreatie, urging the many inconveniences that might follow so wicked and wilfull proceedings, as the imminent daunger of himselfe and his estate. The future harmes that might betide others by his obstinate beginnings, the shame that ensues, such a fact, the wronges done to the power, and authoritie of his King and Countrie. But head-strong follye, that hath still her rod tyed at her owne Girdle, would not suffer his perswasions to prevaile, his wordes were spoken to deafe eares, and to such a one as neither regarded justice nor authoritie.

So resolutely did this Rebell persist in this outrage, that detaining Captaine *Hart* prisoner, hee forc'd his wife (with some of his owne people appointed to accompany her to that bloodie purpose) to goe to the Forte, whome the Souldiers no sooner espyed but they presently opened the Gates and let her in, laying a side all doubt and suspition of Treacherie, because their Captaines wife was in company, and by this the Souldiers were untimelye brought to their endes: For the Rebells (the Gates being open) rusht violentlye uppon such as kept the Forte, and taking the Castle, put them all to the sword, reserving none alive save the Captaine, his wife and Children. There is no good nature, that beholding on a common Stage any Tragedie, wherein bee represented the miseries of any one man, or the ruine or desolation of
a whole

Newes from Ireland.

a whole Countrie, will not accompanye the outward motions of the Actors, with some inward affection, yea, sometime with teares and vehement compassion, which if wee doe in a Play, whereof the matter is manytimes untrue, and but invented, Then the practises and horrible cruelties of this *Carey Adoughertie* and his associates, even upon our Countriemen, their tormenting, murthering them, and putting them to death, ought much more to move us to commiseration. If we greve when we see cruelties set forth in plaies, because the like have either happened to us heretofore, or may betide us hereafter, Then not onely good cause to lament and be sory for the untimely endes of those silly soules, but to feare also what may follow and happen to others by the like rebellious *Tirrannie*, and Irish inhumanitie, If their cruell courses bee not cut of and prevented by severe Justice and authoritie.

This not all the mischiefe and miserie that the Irish inflicted upon our Souldiers: but as the winde cannot be tyed within a quarter, the Sunne bee shadowed within a Vale, nor oyle bee hidden in water, So this poyson of Rebellion swelling their mindes to further mischiefe, could not be long contained, but it must needs breake out in more ulcerous falsehood and treacherie: for as one stormie clowde in the Firmament is seconded by another, and as one Beacon burning sets another on fire, so in this undutifull and unnaturall tumult of the Irish, one out-rage begets another.

For this barbarous cruelty committed thus over night that was able to have made any relenting mens feet to have stumbled, their eyes to have dazeled, their hearts quaked, & their bodies trembled when they went about to effect it, was yet seconded with a worse then that, even the very next morning following,

Newes from Ireland

following, so restles were their desires in the pursuite of mischeif, so obdurate their hearts in doing violence, & their feet so ready to carrie them to further villany, that they stood not long to pause in their divelish purpose. But about two of the clocke in the morning, made hast to the Derry, which is some two miles from the Castle of this Sir *Carey Adougherty*: There having company appointed to be assistant in this bloody practise, it was not long before they had taken both the towne and Forte, and made such a generall havocke, that the fight might have seemed able to stir mercie even in the moste tyrannicall disposition.

But in them there was neither sparke of pittie nor pyetie, so much were their mutinous mindes led away with a thirstie desire of blood, that a man beholding their mercilesse proceedings, might thinke that the soules of such men lay buried in their sences, and that their conceipts of their present crueltie had utterly confounded in them, the consideration of what might happen to themselves.

They took also the Bishop of the Derry his wife & Family prisoners, the Bishop at that time being at Dublin in Ireland: The surprizing of this Town and Fort was not all the miserie or mischiefe that was wrought by this mutinous storme, but as it is the nature of fortune to be sildome times singuler, either in her frownes or favours, but that one is commonly heaped on the necke of another.

So it hapned in this bloody stratageme, for the Towne of Derrie & the Fort being taken, there succeeded another evill, worse then the first. These cruell and disloyall spirits (that have not yet failed to shew themselves a lewde rebellious generation) having gotten the upper hand by their treacherie, did not spare to followe their disobedience with such bloody pursuite, that they put to sword, the governour
Sir

Newes from Ireland

Paulet, with his friends, Souldiers and associates, and continued to doe such further mischiefe, that they were not content to murther the people, but they first ransackt the Towne, tooke their goods and their houses, and consumed the whole Towne into Cynders and ashes.

And now the said Rebell Sir *Carey Adoughertie* is besiedging of the *Leffierd* aforesaide. Such is the corruption of humaine conditions, that it more easily lends a helping hand to propogate matter of mischiefe, then to restraine an evill action pretended.

Sir *Carey Adoughartie* had no sooner set foote forward to his blody enterprise, but he had many followers to assist him in his wicked proceedings: amongst whome *Felli Me Reeah Mack Davy*, a notable seditious person of that countrie is by proclamation from the Lord Deputy of Ireland, and his honourable counsell, worthely branded with the name of Rebell, who is at this time aiding the said Sir *Carey* with his best might to take the *Lefferd*.

How be it as treacherous beginnings have still failed in the events and expectations, so no doubt but although the *Lefferd* be now much threatned and indangered by the said Rebells, who continually attempt her overthrowe, yet the worthinesse and loyall industrie of such as are imployed by his Majestie, for her releefe, shall prevaile against all Irish treacherie; as namely the grounded knowledge and experience of Sir *Ralph Bingley*, who hath his imployment by Sea, to dashe their daring presumption. And also the honorable care of Sir *Oliver Lambert*, and Sir *Rich: Wingfield* by land, whose forwardnes so well knowne in other matters heeretofore committed to their care, gives good hope of prosperous successe for the present imployment.

FINIS

NEWES
From Lough-foyle
in *Ireland*.
Of the late treacherous Action
and rebellion of Sir Carey Adougherty *and* Felli Me Reeah Mack
Davy.
With his ransacking and burning of the
Cittie of Derry &c.
And the inhumane murther of Sir George Paulet, his associates, and most of the inhabitants
of the Derry aforesaid.

LONDON
Printed for Nathaniell Butter, and are to be
solde at his shop in Paules Church-yard,
neere Saint Austens Gate
1608

NEWES
From *Lough-foyle* in *Ireland*:
OF
The late treacherous Attempt of
that Rebell Sir Carey Adougherty,
with his ransacking, and burning
of the Citie of Derry.

AS in the naturall body of man there is no forme or constitution so excellent and perfit, but hath in it some taste of corrupt humors, to disturbe and deface the workmanship of nature, So in the politicke body of a Kingdome or common-wealth, there is no government, though never so well managed and setled, but hath still bred in it some corrupt Male-contents, and Maligners of the State:
nor

Newes from Lough-foyle

nor that any countrie is so subject thereunto as that of *Ireland,* appeares by recordes left from former ages, which the condition of the present times confirme.

The happie Raigne of the late deceased Queen of famous memorie, How was it not onely traduced by the calumnious tongues of Catholickes, and all the Popish crew, But her life also so often endangered, that not a yeare past without some notable and divelish plot and project, which neverthelesse by God his especiall power and grace did still faile in the execution? But above all, that hellish and abhorred Treason, which in the third yeare of his Majesties raigne, was so cunningly and dangerously contrived, both against the head and principall members of the Kingdome, did so farre excell all comparison, that unto strange nations the report thereof hath yet scarse entred the compasse of beleife: the effecting whereof had prepared miserie for the childe unborne.

Oh that the wombe of a Country should beare such prodigious monsters, and that the aire of any Climate should give them breath, that like the Earth-borne brethren, envying each others shape, devoures another. For the unquiet minde of man never content with his owne estate, doth passe through all sortes of opinions, and purposes, untill she hath settled the ground of her device, which if

it

in Ireland.

it be framed in the webbe of mischiefe, oh what a work doth it produce so contrary to the quiet nature of man that no single eye or well disposed heart but doth abhor it? This discontentment of minde or rather unreasonable & ambitious desire of glory, is a vice that seduceth the hearts of many subjects from their loyal & duetiful obedience, and fights against modesty, which is a part of temperance. For the modest man (as *Aristotle* saith) desireth honour, as hee ought, & as becommeth him: but he that desireth it by unlawful meanes, is ambitious & carried away with a perturbation of intemperance. Of such as these, there are many exmples, both in sacred and prophane Histories (which may instruct and warne loyall Subjects: Amongst whom commeth here to my remembrance, the notable storie of *Korah* that seditious Herald, and ambitious minded Israelite, whose rebellion, *Moses* at large setteth down with his bad successe and strange punishment. In which ambition (as commonly it falleth out with men infected with that vice) there was first mal-contentment of minde, who not satisfied with that honour & calling wherin he was placed, raised up disquietnes & disturbance among the people. Secondly, there was in him an envious affection, wherby he disdained that *Moses* and *Aaron* should have any power over him. Thirdly, like our vile Anabaptists, he went about to suppresse government, & wold have al to be

of

Newes from Lough-foyle

of equall power and condition, which is the confusion of all estates of people. Fourthly, he raised up open sedition and Rebellion against Governors appointed of God. Fiftly, he went about to have brought the high Priest-hood, from *Aaron* unto himselfe, although hee found fault with others for the same. The holy Scriptures are full of examples, both of Ambitious proceedings, and of the deserved fall and ruine of such unnaturall and undutifull intendments: so like wise are prophane histories.

As what but Ambition stird up *Cæsar* and *Pompey*, *Marcus* and *Silla*, *Octavius*, *Antonius*, & *Lepidus*, by force of armes to put their Countrie to sworde and fire, and so unnaturally to impaire the large & greate scope of the Romaine Empire? What but ambition and discontentment of minde hath drawn many desperate people from time to time not onely to cast out words of disdaine against the honorable rule & reverance of the higher powers, but to forsake their loyall and bounden dueties, and (without any compunction of conscience) to practise the subversion of King, Common-wealth, and Countrie.

I neede not enlarge my selfe in this matter, either by divine or prophane examples: our home-bred experience and testimonie, may serve from time to time to expresse the follyes of such ambitious persons, as have beene led either by envie or presumption

in Ireland.

sumption, to lift up hand against their head, and so worke their owne falles and fatall destructions. To set aside the Treasonable practises of discontented Papists, & other malevolent opposites to the Sate, Many other commotions and insurrections of the giddie-headed and ungoverned people, uppon false and fained pretexts and suggestions, having alwaies bene without ground in the foundation, have likewise bene without forme in the building: So dissonant to the well tuned peace & tranquility of the Land, that many times it hath mard that goodly consent and harmony, wherewith both heaven and earth is delighted. Such was the rebellion of *Jack Straw* and *Wat Tyler* in the daies of Richard the second at that time when in his minoritie, hee gat a singuler hope and expectation of a happie raigne & government. The like in the time of *Henry* the sixt, by *Jack Cade*, that assumed the name of *Mortimer* in the disturbance of the peaceable condition of his Raigne which though it had a ground and project, plotted by the Duke of *Yorke*, that then made a claime, and title to the Crowne, and happily from him a countenance assisting thereunto, yet were the proceedings mishapen, & the successe answerable.

Kets commotion in Norfolk in the raigne of *Edward* the sixt, a moste excellent Prince, being without just cause, or colour either of their own greevances, or the Kings government, did in a short time

growe

Newes from Lough-foyle

growe to such a body, but so horrid & monstrous, that at this day there are misshapen monuments left of that prodigious Rebellion. The rebellyon of *Tyrone* in *Ireland*, in the daies of her late majesties happie raigne, how monstrous was it in respect of the mischiefes it brought with it, and left behinde it? How unnaturall in respect of the many miseries and untimely deathes that it wrought, even to his owne Countriemen? how unthankfull in respect of the manifolde favours hee reeceived at the handes of his Soveraigne, to whome hee worthily owed his deerest blood, his life, and all that ever he enjoyed?

But the endes of all such as have practised Rebellion, who is so ignorant that he hath not either read or heard them, or so voide of understanding, that he cannot prejudicate of their successe, and fith in this case there is occasion present ministred to write (though I could be content my penne were rather idle then busied in the treatye of such a subject) I have thought good, so farre as my instructions lead me, to make knowne to the world the nature and manner of the late moste cruell and unnaturall proceedings of some of *Tyrone* his accomplices in *Ireland*, upon the bodyes of divers of his Majesties faithfull and loving Subjects: in setting downe of which infamous Actes and attempts of murther & treason, I shall labour to exhort all well disposed
Subjects

in Ireland.

Subjects to the duetie of obedience, and exhort al factious and turbulent spirits from the treasonable and ill relisht poyson of Rebellion, that being once distasted in the pallate of conceit, it may hereafter not infect the heart with consent: And I do much wonder that reasonable men should in this case be much worse then insensible creatures: the one still naturally striving to preserve, and the other unnaturally to destroy their kinde: and if they would but rightly examine the qualitie and condition of times past, together with the nature of murther, Treason, and rebellions, they should soone finde that as the successe hath failed them in their expectations, so their punishments have still suted to their deservements, and that justly too, for where offence is but tollerated by authoritie, or incouraged by impunitie, There insolencie and mens misbehaviours commaund the Law, which is the greatest error (I suppose) that can be in government.

So preposterous and out of order are the devices and attempts of Rebellion and treacherie, that such as are misled by their directions, doe never measure their owne actions by Time, or their affections by discretion, but in head-strong & improvident course, undertake and prosecute their rash and heedeles enterprises, oftentimes to the ruine and destruction of themselves and many others.

Newes from Lough-foyle

others. But above all, this late cruell and bloudy plot, practised about *Lough-foyle* in *Ireland*, as it ought with all pietie to bee pittied, so deserves it to be remembred, as a demonstrance of the Irish inhumanitie: who notwithstanding his majesties lenitie and many gratious favours towards them, have still continued their wilfull & bloudie courses, without any just cause or ground, what colour soever they set upon it, to face the garment of their rebellion, Their hearts being so obdurate & inclined to mischiefe, that they quite forget to understand how unlawfull and undutifull their actions are, How offensive to God and to the King, aswell in the duties of devotion as obedience, how hurtfull in regard of example to others, how hopelesse in regard of successe to themselves, how daungerous in respect of their states present, and how infamous in the consideration of times to come: when (notwithstanding the best glosse and colour they can set uppon their attempts) they shal yet in after times (as others have done in former) carrye the verye names and faces of Traitors, and march in the hated rankes of *Jacke Straw*, *Wat Tyler*, *Jacke Cade* and others, being marked with the odious and detestable brand, and stampe of Rebels.

This *Lough-foyle* is a River in the North part of *Ireland*, bounded on the one side with the countrie of *Ocane* and *Tyrone*, and on the other, with the

Land

in Ireland.

Landes and living of *Oddonnell* and of Sir *Carey Adougherty*, a Rebell by whome this late murther and Treacherie was chieflie plotted and prosecuted: It is adjoyning to the Ilands betweene *Scotland* and *Ireland*, and about some eight yeares since or somewhat more in the time of the great rebellion, this place was surprised and taken by the worthy knight Sir *Henry Dockwray*, whose first landing was at *Kilmore*, about twelve miles of the right hand of the River within the Country, & then country of Sir *John Adoughertie* (father of this Sir *Carey*) who was at that time living. Here Sir *Henrie Dockwray*, found a Castle against the River aforesaide, which he very sufficiently fortified, and afterwards made a strong Forte there called *Kilmore*.

Within one moneth following, he went three miles beyond that, and took the *Derry* without any resistance, lying upon the said River of *Loughfoyle*, where is since erected a goodly Town called the Citie of the *Derry*, and where also he built two Fortes, and a goodly house.

After this, he made another Forte called *Dun a Longe*, a place some three miles beyond that, on the left hand of the River, and then the *Leffierd* some xij miles beyond the *Derrie*.

But changes and alterations are (for the most parte) full of perills and daunger, and then mischaunces doe soonest befall us, when wee accounte

our

Newes from Lough-foyle

our selves most secure, and are best perswaded of our safety: as happened to Sir *George Paulet* of Hampshier, who went into *Ireland* with his wife and children, and was made Governour of the *Derry* aforesaid, by the assignement of Sir *Henry Dockewray*, the which place Sir *Henry* had formerly obtained in the time of warre, by his owne valour and industry.

But to satisfie the Readers expectations of the trecherous attempts of Sir *Cary Adougherty* aforesaid, which is the onely purpose of this present relation, you shall understand, that as the Serpent never stings more deadly, then when hee bites without hissing, so an enimie never intends more deepe mischeife and villany, then when he shaddowes his purposes under the shewe and pretexte of friendship and amitie.

In what bloody manner dealt *Joab* with *Abner*? when he pretended to speake peaceably with him in the gate? concerning which trecherous manner *David* left order with *Salomon* his sonne, to which *Salomon* agreed, and cause *Benaiah* to smite *Joab*, having caught holde on the hornes of the Altar, and there hee died.

In what trecherous manner have many Hipocrites made Feasts, and in the middest of their cuppes imbrued their hands with blood? To omit the butchery of *Abimilech*, uppon his brethren

for

in Ireland.

for the placing himselfe in the Kingdome: to o-mite the poisoning of King *John*, King of *England* by a Moncke of Swinsthead Abbey: the murther fresh in memory, done by a Frier most bouldly upon *Henry* the late King of *France*: the villanous attompte uppon the Prince of *Orrenge*: To passe over the abhominable crueltie of the *Guizians*, bathing themselves in blood in the time of the massacre: and that practise against the Lord *Chastillon*, the Lord high Admirall of *France*: And to omite to speake of *Bothwell* his villany, not any waye inferiour, or behinde the rest in savage crueltie, for his treason against our King his most excellent Majestie: this un-heard of manner of treacherie, contrived and effected by Sir *Cary Adougherty*, is, for the exercise as monstrous, and for the execution, as cruell and tiranous as any that is or can be mentioned.

Hee made shew and protestation of great love and friendship he beare to Captaine *Hart*, who was left commaunder of the Forte and Castle of Kill-more, but under the cloake and habite of amity, he shrowded the hate and heart of enemie.

Simulata æquitas, non est æquitas, sed duplex iniquitas, quia iniquitas est & similatio: fained equitie is no equitie, but a double iniquitie, because it is iniquitie and dissimulation: Such a one hath this
Irish

Newes from Lough-foyle

Irishe rebell shewed him selfe. *Intus Nero, foris Cato:* In shew, grave as *Cato*, and friendly as a Senatour: in heart as cruell as *Nero*, and as tirannous as a thirstie blood-sucker: As a beast compact of many beasts, According to the Poets saying, *Leo pars prima, Draco media Ipsa Chimera:* The principall and fore-part a Lyon, the middle part a Dragon, A very Chymera it selfe: Such a one is hee as *Salomon* speaketh of, that invites a man to his table in shew of curtesye, and meanes him mischeife, that offers himselfe in renewing of friendship to eate and drinke with a man, and as though hee said in his heart, eate and drincke, but his heart is not with thee.

Such a one was *Judas*, who accompaining Christ as his Disciple, eating and drinking with him, did yet with a *Judas* kisse betray him: and such a one (I say) is this rebel Sir *Carey Adougherty*: hee made greate shewe of love to Captaine *Hart*, but it was not with his heart, for he harboured an inward and secret rancour and malice, whereof he meant ere long to give open signe and outward demonstration, as it thus happened.

This Sir *Carey* being a great Alderman, of the Citty of *Derry*, in Aprill last past, invited Captaine *Hart* to dinner, with his wife and children, and feasted them very long, and that in such costly and sumpteous manner, as their extraordinary

and

in Ireland.

and kinde entertainement for the present, and the long under-hand love, that hee formerly pretended to shewe to the Captaine, did quite remove al feare & suspition of any treacherie to follow. But no sooner did nights approaching summon this Captain *Hart* & his company home to his charge, and he began to take his leave, and to give heartie thankes for the entertainment he had received, but Sir *Carey Adougherty* changed the coppie of his countenance, told him that this was but a traine to entrap him, & a faire & sweet beginning to drawe on a foule and shrap conclusion, and with that laid hands upon him, and tooke him prisoner.

This strooke colde to the Captaines heart, yet at first he thought it but a forme of feare put upon him in jest, but when hee perceived by the continuance both of this Rebel his stern behaviour and countenance, that it was past jest, and a purpose practised in good earnest.

Seeing no other remedie, hee began to fall to intreatie, urging the many inconveniences, that might followe so wicked and wilfull proceedings, As the imminent daunger of himselfe and his estate, The future harmes that might betide others by his obstinate beginnings, the shame that ensues such a fact, the wronges done to the power and authoritie of his King and Countrie. But headstrong folly that hath still her rod tyed at her owne
girdle,

Newes from Lough-foyle

girdle, would not suffer his perswasions to prevaile, his wordes were spoken to deafe eares, & to such a one as neither regarded justice nor authoritie.

So resolutelye did this Rebell persist in this outrage, that detaining Captaine *Hart* prisoner, hee forc'd his wife (with some of his own people appointed to accompany her to that bloudie purpose) to goe to the Forte, whome the Souldiers no sooner espyed but they presently opened the Gates and let her in, laying aside all doubt and suspition of Treacherie, because their Captaines wife was in companye, and by this the Souldyers were untimelye brought to their endes: For the rebels (the Gates being open) rusht violentlye uppon such as kept the Forte, and taking the Castle, put them all to the sword, reserving none alive, Save the Captain, his wife and chilldren.

There is no good nature, that beholding on a common Stage anye Tragedie, wherein bee represented the misteries of any one man, or the ruine or desolation of a whole Countrie, will not accompanye the outward motions of the Actors, with some inward affection, yea, sometime with teares and vehement compassion, which if we doe in a play, whereof the matter is many times untrue, and but invented, Then
the

in Ireland.

 the practises and horrible cruelties of this *Carey Adougherty* and his associates, even uppon our Countrimen, their tormenting, murthering them, and putting them to death, ought much more to move us to commiseration: If wee greeve when we see cruelties set forth in plaies, because the like have either hapned to us heretofore, or may betide us hereafter, Then not onely good cause to lament and be sorry for the untimely endes of those silly soules, but to feare also what may follow and happen to others by the like rebellious Tyrannie, and Irish inhumanitie, If their cruell courses bee not cut off and prevented by severe Justice and authority.

 This is not al the mischief & miserie that the Irish inflicted upon our Souldiers: but as the winde cannot bee tyed within a quarter, the Sunne bee shadowed within a Vale, nor oyle be hidden in Water, So this poyson of Rebellion swelling their mindes to further mischiefe, could not bee long contained, but it must needes breake out into more ulcerous falshoode and treacherie: for as one stormie clowde in the Firmament is seconded by another, and as one Beacon burning sets another on fire, so in this undutifull and unnaturall tumult of the Irish, one out-rage begets another.

 For this barbarous cruelty committed this over
night

Newes from Lough-foyle

night that was able to have made any relenting mens feet to have stumpled, their eyes to have dazeled, their hearts quaked, & their bodies trembled when they went about to effect it, was yet seconded with a worse then that, even the verie next morning following, so restles were their desires in the pursuite of mischiefe so obdurate their hearts in dooing violence, and their feete so ready to carrie them to further villanie, that they stood not long to pause on their divelish purpose. But about two of the clocke in the morning, made haste to the *Derry* which is some two miles from the Castle of this Sir *Carey Adoughertie*: There having company appointed to be aisistant in this bloody practise, it was not long before they had taken both the town and Forte, and made such a general havock, that the sight might have seemed able to stirre mercie even in the moste Tyrannicall disposition.

But in them there was neither sparke of pittye nor pietie, so much were their mutinous mindes led away with a thirstie desire of blood, that a man beholding their mercilesse proceedings, might think that the soules of such men lay buryed in their sences, and that their conceipts of their present crueltie had utterly confounded in them, the consideration of what might happen to themselves.

They took also the bishop of the *Derry* his wife & family Prisoners, the Bishop at that time beeing at
Dublin

in Ireland.

Dublin in *Ireland.*

The surprizing of this Towne and Forte was not all the miserie or mischiefe that was wrought by this mutinous storme, but as it is the nature of Fortune to be seldome times singuler, either in her frownes or favours, but that one is commonly heaped on the necke of another.

So it hapned in this bloody stratageme, for the Towne of *Derry*, and the Forte being taken, there succeeded another evill, worse then the first. These cruell and disloyall spirits (that have not yet failed to shew themselves a lewde rebellious generation) having gotten the upper hand by their treacherie, did not spare to followe their disobedience with such bloody pursuite that they put to sword, the Governour Sir *George Paulet*, with his wife, Souldiers and whole family, and continued to do such further mischiefe, that they were not content to murther the people, but they first ransackt the Towne, tooke their goods and their houses, and consumed the whole Towne into Cynders and ashes. And now the said Rebell Sir *Carey Adoughertie* is besiedging of the *Leffierd* aforesaid.

Oh that such kinde of pepole would but enter into the name and nature of Rebellion, and the punishments due to the fame, that remembring
the

Newes from Lough-foyle

the ugly & haynous enormities of the one, & the
severitie of the other, they may learne to
imbrace due obedience, & not mark
their posteritie with the name of
rebels by inconsiderate and
wicked attempts & by so
many factious com-
motions and con-
spiracies.

FINIS.